50 Wholesome Breakfast Bowls for a Healthy Start

By: Kelly Johnson

Table of Contents

- Classic Acai Bowl with Granola & Berries
- Greek Yogurt & Honey Bowl with Walnuts
- Peanut Butter & Banana Oatmeal Bowl
- Chia Pudding Bowl with Mango & Coconut
- Overnight Oats with Almond Butter & Chia Seeds
- Protein-Packed Quinoa Breakfast Bowl
- Green Smoothie Bowl with Spinach & Avocado
- Warm Apple Cinnamon Oatmeal Bowl
- Mixed Berry & Flaxseed Yogurt Bowl
- Pumpkin Spice Oatmeal Bowl with Pecans
- Almond Butter & Dark Chocolate Banana Bowl
- Golden Turmeric Oatmeal Bowl
- Savory Quinoa & Egg Breakfast Bowl
- Strawberry & Coconut Chia Pudding Bowl
- Mango & Pineapple Smoothie Bowl
- Matcha Green Tea Yogurt Bowl with Hemp Seeds
- Carrot Cake Oatmeal Bowl with Walnuts
- Cashew Butter & Cacao Nib Bowl
- Vanilla Chia Pudding with Roasted Almonds
- Raspberry & Almond Butter Overnight Oats
- Banana & Pecan Warm Quinoa Bowl
- Blueberry & Macadamia Nut Smoothie Bowl
- Sweet Potato & Cinnamon Oatmeal Bowl
- Chocolate & Hazelnut Chia Pudding Bowl
- Cottage Cheese & Honey Bowl with Figs
- Banana Bread-Inspired Oatmeal Bowl
- Wild Rice & Maple Pecan Breakfast Bowl
- Avocado & Egg Protein Breakfast Bowl
- Blackberry & Tahini Yogurt Bowl
- Roasted Peach & Almond Oatmeal Bowl
- Mocha Smoothie Bowl with Almond Butter
- Fig & Pistachio Quinoa Breakfast Bowl
- Chai-Spiced Oatmeal with Cashews
- Tropical Dragon Fruit & Coconut Bowl
- Apple Pie Overnight Oats Bowl

- Savory Chickpea & Spinach Breakfast Bowl
- Cranberry Orange Oatmeal Bowl
- Roasted Pear & Cinnamon Yogurt Bowl
- Chocolate Banana Chia Pudding Bowl
- Avocado & Smoked Salmon Power Bowl
- Blueberry & Coconut Kefir Bowl
- Nutty Granola Bowl with Yogurt & Berries
- Roasted Sweet Potato & Kale Breakfast Bowl
- Black Forest Smoothie Bowl with Dark Chocolate
- Zucchini Bread Oatmeal Bowl
- Kiwi & Lime Chia Pudding Bowl
- Cherry & Almond Overnight Oats
- Maple Walnut Greek Yogurt Bowl
- Pomegranate & Pistachio Quinoa Bowl
- Fresh Citrus & Honey Breakfast Bowl

Classic Açaí Bowl with Granola & Berries

Ingredients:

- 1 frozen açaí packet
- 1/2 frozen banana
- 1/2 cup almond milk
- 1/2 cup mixed berries (strawberries, blueberries, raspberries)
- 1/4 cup granola
- 1 tbsp honey

Instructions:

1. Blend açaí, banana, and almond milk until smooth.
2. Pour into a bowl and top with berries, granola, and honey.

Greek Yogurt & Honey Bowl with Walnuts

Ingredients:

- 1 cup Greek yogurt
- 1 tbsp honey
- 1/4 cup walnuts, chopped
- 1/2 tsp cinnamon

Instructions:

1. Spoon yogurt into a bowl.
2. Drizzle with honey and sprinkle with walnuts and cinnamon.

Peanut Butter & Banana Oatmeal Bowl

Ingredients:

- 1 cup rolled oats
- 2 cups milk or water
- 1 tbsp peanut butter
- 1 banana, sliced
- 1 tbsp honey

Instructions:

1. Cook oats in milk or water.
2. Stir in peanut butter and top with banana slices.
3. Drizzle with honey before serving.

Chia Pudding Bowl with Mango & Coconut

Ingredients:

- 1/4 cup chia seeds
- 1 cup coconut milk
- 1 tbsp honey
- 1/2 cup diced mango
- 2 tbsp shredded coconut

Instructions:

1. Mix chia seeds, coconut milk, and honey.
2. Refrigerate overnight, then top with mango and shredded coconut.

Overnight Oats with Almond Butter & Chia Seeds

Ingredients:

- 1/2 cup rolled oats
- 1 tbsp chia seeds
- 1/2 cup almond milk
- 1 tbsp almond butter
- 1 tbsp maple syrup

Instructions:

1. Combine all ingredients in a jar and mix well.
2. Refrigerate overnight and stir before serving.

Protein-Packed Quinoa Breakfast Bowl

Ingredients:

- 1/2 cup cooked quinoa
- 1/2 cup Greek yogurt
- 1 tbsp flaxseeds
- 1/2 cup mixed berries
- 1 tbsp honey

Instructions:

1. Cook quinoa and let cool slightly.
2. Mix with yogurt and top with flaxseeds, berries, and honey.

Green Smoothie Bowl with Spinach & Avocado

Ingredients:

- 1 frozen banana
- 1/2 avocado
- 1/2 cup spinach
- 1/2 cup almond milk
- 1 tbsp chia seeds
- 1/4 cup granola

Instructions:

1. Blend banana, avocado, spinach, and almond milk until smooth.
2. Pour into a bowl and top with chia seeds and granola.

Warm Apple Cinnamon Oatmeal Bowl

Ingredients:

- 1 cup rolled oats
- 2 cups milk or water
- 1/2 cup diced apples
- 1/2 tsp cinnamon
- 1 tbsp maple syrup

Instructions:

1. Cook oats in milk or water.
2. Stir in apples, cinnamon, and maple syrup.

Mixed Berry & Flaxseed Yogurt Bowl

Ingredients:

- 1 cup Greek yogurt
- 1/2 cup mixed berries
- 1 tbsp ground flaxseeds
- 1 tbsp honey

Instructions:

1. Spoon yogurt into a bowl.
2. Top with berries, flaxseeds, and honey.

Pumpkin Spice Oatmeal Bowl with Pecans

Ingredients:

- 1 cup rolled oats
- 2 cups milk or water
- 1/4 cup pumpkin purée
- 1/2 tsp pumpkin spice
- 1 tbsp maple syrup
- 2 tbsp chopped pecans

Instructions:

1. Cook oats in milk or water.
2. Stir in pumpkin purée, pumpkin spice, and maple syrup.
3. Top with chopped pecans before serving.

Almond Butter & Dark Chocolate Banana Bowl

Ingredients:

- 1 banana, sliced
- 2 tbsp almond butter
- 1 tbsp dark chocolate chips
- 1/4 cup granola

Instructions:

1. Arrange banana slices in a bowl.
2. Drizzle with almond butter and sprinkle with dark chocolate chips and granola.

Golden Turmeric Oatmeal Bowl

Ingredients:

- 1 cup rolled oats
- 2 cups almond milk
- 1/2 tsp turmeric
- 1/4 tsp cinnamon
- 1/4 tsp black pepper
- 1 tbsp honey
- 2 tbsp toasted coconut flakes

Instructions:

1. Cook oats in almond milk.
2. Stir in turmeric, cinnamon, black pepper, and honey.
3. Top with toasted coconut flakes before serving.

Savory Quinoa & Egg Breakfast Bowl

Ingredients:

- 1/2 cup cooked quinoa
- 1 fried or poached egg
- 1/4 avocado, sliced
- 1 tbsp feta cheese
- 1 tbsp fresh parsley

Instructions:

1. Assemble quinoa in a bowl.
2. Top with a fried egg, avocado slices, feta, and parsley.

Strawberry & Coconut Chia Pudding Bowl

Ingredients:

- 1/4 cup chia seeds
- 1 cup coconut milk
- 1 tbsp honey
- 1/2 cup sliced strawberries
- 2 tbsp shredded coconut

Instructions:

1. Mix chia seeds, coconut milk, and honey.
2. Refrigerate overnight, then top with strawberries and shredded coconut.

Mango & Pineapple Smoothie Bowl

Ingredients:

- 1/2 cup frozen mango
- 1/2 cup frozen pineapple
- 1/2 cup coconut milk
- 1 tbsp chia seeds
- 1/4 cup granola

Instructions:

1. Blend mango, pineapple, and coconut milk until smooth.
2. Pour into a bowl and top with chia seeds and granola.

Matcha Green Tea Yogurt Bowl with Hemp Seeds

Ingredients:

- 1 cup Greek yogurt
- 1 tsp matcha powder
- 1 tbsp honey
- 1 tbsp hemp seeds

Instructions:

1. Mix yogurt with matcha powder and honey.
2. Top with hemp seeds before serving.

Carrot Cake Oatmeal Bowl with Walnuts

Ingredients:

- 1 cup rolled oats
- 2 cups milk or water
- 1/2 cup shredded carrots
- 1/2 tsp cinnamon
- 1 tbsp honey
- 2 tbsp chopped walnuts

Instructions:

1. Cook oats in milk or water.
2. Stir in shredded carrots, cinnamon, and honey.
3. Top with walnuts before serving.

Cashew Butter & Cacao Nib Bowl

Ingredients:

- 1 banana, sliced
- 2 tbsp cashew butter
- 1 tbsp cacao nibs
- 1/4 cup granola

Instructions:

1. Arrange banana slices in a bowl.
2. Drizzle with cashew butter and sprinkle with cacao nibs and granola.

Vanilla Chia Pudding with Roasted Almonds

Ingredients:

- 1/4 cup chia seeds
- 1 cup almond milk
- 1/2 tsp vanilla extract
- 1 tbsp honey or maple syrup
- 2 tbsp roasted almonds, chopped

Instructions:

1. Mix chia seeds, almond milk, vanilla extract, and honey.
2. Refrigerate overnight.
3. Top with roasted almonds before serving.

Raspberry & Almond Butter Overnight Oats

Ingredients:

- 1/2 cup rolled oats
- 1 tbsp chia seeds
- 1/2 cup almond milk
- 1 tbsp almond butter
- 1/4 cup fresh raspberries
- 1 tsp maple syrup

Instructions:

1. Mix oats, chia seeds, and almond milk in a jar.
2. Refrigerate overnight.
3. Stir in almond butter and top with raspberries and maple syrup before serving.

Banana & Pecan Warm Quinoa Bowl

Ingredients:

- 1/2 cup cooked quinoa
- 1/2 cup milk or almond milk
- 1/2 banana, sliced
- 1 tbsp maple syrup
- 2 tbsp chopped pecans

Instructions:

1. Heat quinoa with milk over medium heat.
2. Stir in banana slices and maple syrup.
3. Top with pecans before serving.

Blueberry & Macadamia Nut Smoothie Bowl

Ingredients:

- 1/2 cup frozen blueberries
- 1 frozen banana
- 1/2 cup coconut milk
- 1 tbsp chia seeds
- 2 tbsp chopped macadamia nuts

Instructions:

1. Blend blueberries, banana, and coconut milk until smooth.
2. Pour into a bowl and top with chia seeds and macadamia nuts.

Sweet Potato & Cinnamon Oatmeal Bowl

Ingredients:

- 1 cup rolled oats
- 2 cups milk or water
- 1/2 cup mashed sweet potato
- 1/2 tsp cinnamon
- 1 tbsp maple syrup
- 1 tbsp chopped pecans

Instructions:

1. Cook oats in milk or water.
2. Stir in mashed sweet potato, cinnamon, and maple syrup.
3. Top with chopped pecans before serving.

Chocolate & Hazelnut Chia Pudding Bowl

Ingredients:

- 1/4 cup chia seeds
- 1 cup almond milk
- 1 tbsp cocoa powder
- 1 tbsp maple syrup
- 2 tbsp chopped hazelnuts

Instructions:

1. Mix chia seeds, almond milk, cocoa powder, and maple syrup.
2. Refrigerate overnight.
3. Top with chopped hazelnuts before serving.

Cottage Cheese & Honey Bowl with Figs

Ingredients:

- 1 cup cottage cheese
- 1 tbsp honey
- 2 fresh figs, sliced
- 1 tbsp chopped walnuts

Instructions:

1. Spoon cottage cheese into a bowl.
2. Drizzle with honey and top with figs and walnuts.

Banana Bread-Inspired Oatmeal Bowl

Ingredients:

- 1 cup rolled oats
- 2 cups milk or water
- 1 mashed banana
- 1/2 tsp cinnamon
- 1 tbsp chopped walnuts
- 1 tbsp maple syrup

Instructions:

1. Cook oats in milk or water.
2. Stir in mashed banana, cinnamon, and maple syrup.
3. Top with walnuts before serving.

Wild Rice & Maple Pecan Breakfast Bowl

Ingredients:

- 1/2 cup cooked wild rice
- 1/2 cup almond milk
- 1 tbsp maple syrup
- 2 tbsp chopped pecans
- 1/4 tsp cinnamon

Instructions:

1. Heat wild rice with almond milk and maple syrup.
2. Stir in cinnamon and top with pecans.

Avocado & Egg Protein Breakfast Bowl

Ingredients:

- 1/2 avocado, sliced
- 2 eggs, poached or fried
- 1/2 cup cooked quinoa
- 1 tbsp feta cheese
- 1 tbsp chopped fresh parsley

Instructions:

1. Assemble quinoa in a bowl.
2. Top with avocado slices, poached eggs, and feta.
3. Sprinkle with parsley before serving.

Blackberry & Tahini Yogurt Bowl

Ingredients:

- 1 cup Greek yogurt
- 1/2 cup fresh blackberries
- 1 tbsp tahini
- 1 tbsp honey
- 1 tbsp chia seeds

Instructions:

1. Spoon yogurt into a bowl.
2. Top with blackberries, tahini, and honey.
3. Sprinkle with chia seeds before serving.

Roasted Peach & Almond Oatmeal Bowl

Ingredients:

- 1 cup rolled oats
- 2 cups milk or water
- 1 peach, sliced
- 1 tbsp brown sugar
- 1/4 tsp cinnamon
- 2 tbsp sliced almonds

Instructions:

1. Roast peach slices with brown sugar and cinnamon at **375°F (190°C) for 15 minutes**.
2. Cook oats in milk or water.
3. Top with roasted peaches and sliced almonds before serving.

Mocha Smoothie Bowl with Almond Butter

Ingredients:

- 1 frozen banana
- 1/2 cup cold brew coffee
- 1/2 cup almond milk
- 1 tbsp cocoa powder
- 1 tbsp almond butter
- 1/4 cup granola

Instructions:

1. Blend banana, coffee, almond milk, cocoa powder, and almond butter until smooth.
2. Pour into a bowl and top with granola.

Fig & Pistachio Quinoa Breakfast Bowl

Ingredients:

- 1/2 cup cooked quinoa
- 1/2 cup almond milk
- 2 fresh figs, sliced
- 2 tbsp chopped pistachios
- 1 tbsp honey

Instructions:

1. Warm quinoa with almond milk.
2. Top with figs, pistachios, and honey before serving.

Chai-Spiced Oatmeal with Cashews

Ingredients:

- 1 cup rolled oats
- 2 cups milk or water
- 1/2 tsp chai spice blend
- 1 tbsp honey
- 2 tbsp chopped cashews

Instructions:

1. Cook oats in milk or water.
2. Stir in chai spice blend and honey.
3. Top with cashews before serving.

Tropical Dragon Fruit & Coconut Bowl

Ingredients:

- 1/2 cup frozen dragon fruit
- 1 frozen banana
- 1/2 cup coconut milk
- 1 tbsp shredded coconut
- 1/4 cup granola

Instructions:

1. Blend dragon fruit, banana, and coconut milk until smooth.
2. Pour into a bowl and top with shredded coconut and granola.

Apple Pie Overnight Oats Bowl

Ingredients:

- 1/2 cup rolled oats
- 1/2 cup almond milk
- 1/2 tsp cinnamon
- 1/4 cup diced apples
- 1 tbsp maple syrup
- 1 tbsp chopped walnuts

Instructions:

1. Mix oats, almond milk, cinnamon, and maple syrup.
2. Refrigerate overnight.
3. Stir in apples and walnuts before serving.

Savory Chickpea & Spinach Breakfast Bowl

Ingredients:

- 1/2 cup cooked chickpeas
- 1 cup sautéed spinach
- 1 poached or fried egg
- 1/2 tsp cumin
- 1 tbsp feta cheese

Instructions:

1. Season chickpeas with cumin and warm them.
2. Sauté spinach until wilted.
3. Assemble in a bowl with a poached egg and feta.

Cranberry Orange Oatmeal Bowl

Ingredients:

- 1 cup rolled oats
- 2 cups milk or water
- 1/4 cup dried cranberries
- 1 tsp orange zest
- 1 tbsp honey

Instructions:

1. Cook oats in milk or water.
2. Stir in cranberries, orange zest, and honey before serving.

Roasted Pear & Cinnamon Yogurt Bowl

Ingredients:

- 1 pear, sliced
- 1/2 tsp cinnamon
- 1 tbsp maple syrup
- 1 cup Greek yogurt
- 2 tbsp chopped walnuts

Instructions:

1. Roast pear slices with cinnamon and maple syrup at **375°F (190°C) for 15 minutes**.
2. Spoon yogurt into a bowl and top with roasted pears.
3. Sprinkle with walnuts before serving.

Chocolate Banana Chia Pudding Bowl

Ingredients:

- 1/4 cup chia seeds
- 1 cup almond milk
- 1 tbsp cocoa powder
- 1 tbsp maple syrup
- 1 banana, sliced
- 1 tbsp dark chocolate shavings

Instructions:

1. Mix chia seeds, almond milk, cocoa powder, and maple syrup.
2. Refrigerate overnight.
3. Top with banana slices and dark chocolate shavings before serving.

Avocado & Smoked Salmon Power Bowl

Ingredients:

- 1/2 avocado, sliced
- 2 oz smoked salmon
- 1/2 cup cooked quinoa
- 1 soft-boiled egg
- 1 tbsp capers
- 1 tbsp fresh dill

Instructions:

1. Assemble quinoa, avocado, and smoked salmon in a bowl.
2. Top with a soft-boiled egg, capers, and fresh dill.

Blueberry & Coconut Kefir Bowl

Ingredients:

- 1 cup coconut kefir
- 1/2 cup fresh blueberries
- 1 tbsp shredded coconut
- 1 tbsp honey

Instructions:

1. Pour kefir into a bowl.
2. Top with blueberries, shredded coconut, and honey.

Nutty Granola Bowl with Yogurt & Berries

Ingredients:

- 1 cup Greek yogurt
- 1/2 cup granola
- 1/4 cup mixed berries
- 2 tbsp chopped almonds

Instructions:

1. Spoon yogurt into a bowl.
2. Top with granola, berries, and almonds.

Roasted Sweet Potato & Kale Breakfast Bowl

Ingredients:

- 1/2 cup roasted sweet potatoes
- 1/2 cup sautéed kale
- 1 fried or poached egg
- 1 tbsp feta cheese
- 1/2 tsp paprika

Instructions:

1. Roast sweet potatoes at **400°F (200°C) for 20 minutes**.
2. Sauté kale until wilted.
3. Assemble in a bowl and top with a fried egg, feta, and paprika.

Black Forest Smoothie Bowl with Dark Chocolate

Ingredients:

- 1/2 cup frozen cherries
- 1 frozen banana
- 1/2 cup almond milk
- 1 tbsp cocoa powder
- 1 tbsp dark chocolate shavings
- 1 tbsp granola

Instructions:

1. Blend cherries, banana, almond milk, and cocoa powder until smooth.
2. Pour into a bowl and top with dark chocolate shavings and granola.

Zucchini Bread Oatmeal Bowl

Ingredients:

- 1 cup rolled oats
- 2 cups milk or water
- 1/2 cup shredded zucchini
- 1/2 tsp cinnamon
- 1 tbsp maple syrup
- 2 tbsp chopped walnuts

Instructions:

1. Cook oats in milk or water.
2. Stir in shredded zucchini, cinnamon, and maple syrup.
3. Top with chopped walnuts before serving.

Kiwi & Lime Chia Pudding Bowl

Ingredients:

- 1/4 cup chia seeds
- 1 cup coconut milk
- 1 tbsp honey
- 1 kiwi, sliced
- 1 tsp lime zest

Instructions:

1. Mix chia seeds, coconut milk, and honey.
2. Refrigerate overnight.
3. Top with kiwi slices and lime zest before serving.

Cherry & Almond Overnight Oats

Ingredients:

- 1/2 cup rolled oats
- 1/2 cup almond milk
- 1/2 tsp vanilla extract
- 1/4 cup fresh or dried cherries
- 1 tbsp sliced almonds
- 1 tsp honey

Instructions:

1. Mix oats, almond milk, and vanilla extract in a jar.
2. Refrigerate overnight.
3. Stir in cherries and top with almonds and honey before serving.

Maple Walnut Greek Yogurt Bowl

Ingredients:

- 1 cup Greek yogurt
- 1 tbsp maple syrup
- 2 tbsp chopped walnuts
- 1/2 tsp cinnamon

Instructions:

1. Spoon yogurt into a bowl.
2. Drizzle with maple syrup and sprinkle with walnuts and cinnamon.

Pomegranate & Pistachio Quinoa Bowl

Ingredients:

- 1/2 cup cooked quinoa
- 1/2 cup almond milk
- 2 tbsp pomegranate seeds
- 2 tbsp chopped pistachios
- 1 tbsp honey

Instructions:

1. Warm quinoa with almond milk.
2. Stir in honey and top with pomegranate seeds and pistachios.

Fresh Citrus & Honey Breakfast Bowl

Ingredients:

- 1 orange, segmented
- 1/2 grapefruit, segmented
- 1 tbsp honey
- 1 tbsp chopped mint
- 1 tbsp slivered almonds

Instructions:

1. Arrange citrus segments in a bowl.
2. Drizzle with honey and top with mint and almonds before serving.

www.ingramcontent.com/pod-product-compliance
Lightning Source LLC
LaVergne TN
LVHW081507060526
838201LV00056BA/2980